Gymnastics

Julie Murray

abdopublishing.com

Published by Abdo Kids, a division of ABDO, P.O. Box 398166, Minneapolis, Minnesota 55439.

Abdo Kids Junior™ is a trademark and logo of Abdo Kids.

Printed in the United States of America, North Mankato, Minnesota.

102017

012018

Photo Credits: Alamy, Getty Images, iStock, Shutterstock, ©Pierre-Yves Beaudouin p.22/CC BY-SA 4.0

Production Contributors: Teddy Borth, Jennie Forsberg, Grace Hansen

Design Contributors: Christina Doffing, Candice Keimig, Dorothy Toth

Publisher's Cataloging-in-Publication Data

Names: Murray, Julie, author.

Title: Gymnastics / by Julie Murray.

Description: Minneapolis, Minnesota : Abdo Kids, 2018. | Series: Sports how to |
Includes glossary, index and online resource (page 24).

Identifiers: LCCN 2017908186 | ISBN 9781532104145 (lib.bdg.) | ISBN 9781532105265 (ebook) |
ISBN 9781532105821 (Read-to-me ebook)

Subjects: LCSH: Gymnastics--Juvenile literature. | Gymnastics--Sports & Recreation--Juvenile literature.

Classification: DDC 796.44 --dc23

LC record available at https://lccn.loc.gov/2017908186

Table of Contents

Gymnastics

Ann loves gymnastics! She is ready to go.

Women have 4 events.

Men have 6.

Women's Arena

1. Uneven Bars
2. Floor Exercise Mat
3. Balance Beam
4. Vaulting Table

1. Horizontal Bar
2. Floor Exercise Mat
3. Pommel Horse
4. Rings
5. Parallel Bars
6. Vaulting Table

Judges score the events.

The best score wins!

British Gymnastics
BRITISH GYMNASTICS CHAMPIONSHIPS
#BritGymnastics TWEET FROM YOUR SEAT!

The floor event is 90 seconds. Simone is on the mat. She gets a high score!

USA

Ryan gets chalk. It helps.

His hands won't slip!

Nan is on the **vault**.

She spins in the air.

LONGINES
PEOPLE MAKE GLASGOW
Ford
bp
Virgin media
unicef
GLASGOW 2014
GYMNOVA

Jack trains on the rings.

Asuka is on the beam.

She has good **balance**.

Rio2016

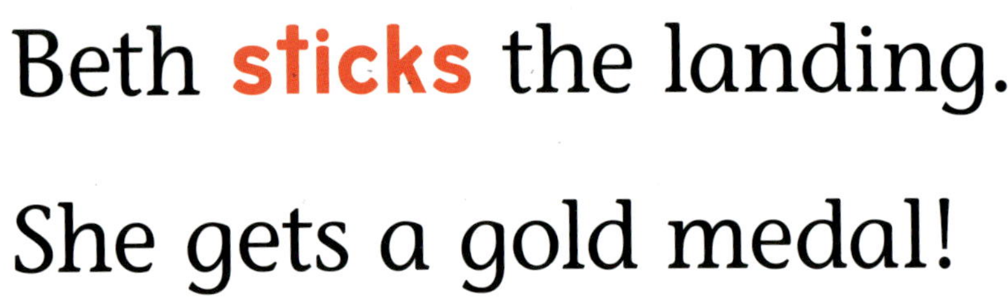

Beth **sticks** the landing.

She gets a gold medal!

Other Gymnastic Events

horizontal bar

parallel bars

pommel horse

uneven bars

Glossary

balance
stay upright and steady.

vault
a running jump over a vaulting horse, usually finishing with an acrobatic dismount.

stick
when a gymnast lands a jump without moving his or her feet.

Index

Visit **abdokids.com** and use this code to access crafts, games, videos, and more!